THE MYSTERY
OF COLLECTIVE
AWAKENING

Questioning Identity and
Connecting in Oneness

JEFF CARREIRA

Other Books in this Series:
The Spiritual Teachings of Jeff Carreira

The Art of Conscious Contentment: A Handbook for Meditation and Spiritual Freedom by Jeff Carreira.

The Gift of Spiritual Abundance: Five Principles for Being Happy and Fulfilled Right Now by Jeff Carreira.

The Experience of Luminous Absorption: The Foundation of Spiritual Life by Jeff Carreira.

Free Resources from Jeff Carreira

Life Without Fear: Meditation as an Antidote to Anxiety with Jeff Carreira. Visit lifewithoutfear.online

Secrets of Profound Meditation: Six Spiritual Insights that will Transform Your Life with Jeff Carreira. Visit secretsofprofoundmeditation.com

Foundations of a New Paradigm: A 6-part program designed to shift the way you experience everything with Jeff Carreira. Visit foundationsofanewparadigm.com

The Mystery of

COLLECTIVE AWAKENING

*Questioning Identity and
Connecting in Oneness*

J EFF C ARREIRA

E MERGENCE E DUCATION

Philadelphia, Pennsylvannia

ISBN: 978-1-954642-16-4

Emergence Education
P.O. Box 63767
Philadelphia, PA 19147
EmergenceEducation.com

Cover and interior design by Sophie Peirce.

Printed in the United States of America.

"You cannot point out one thing that is not here... Everything co-exists... That is why I think the word inter-be should be in the dictionary. "To be" is to inter-be. You cannot just be by yourself alone. You have to inter-be with every other thing.

— THICH NHAT HANH

Contents

Introduction

OVER THE PAST THREE decades there have been two primary practices that have shaped my spiritual path. One was the practice of meditation, which is a solitary practice done in the privacy of inner silence. The other was a practice of what you could call collective or inter-subjective awakening and is composed of different dialog practices generally done in small groups.

Often when we think of spiritual practice we think of practices like meditation or prayer that we do on our own. Alternatively, collective spiritual practices are done with other people and lead to spiritual breakthroughs that are experienced by everyone present. I have written extensively in other books about the practice of meditation, but I have only written once before about collective awakening and that was in my book *The Soul of a New Self.*

In *The Soul of a New Self* I share about a dramatic experience of collective awakening that had a radically transformative impact on my life. It is only in the last chapter of that book that I explain and describe that experience. All of the earlier chapters were used to develop the philosophical and psychological context that I thought would help people understand what the mystery of collective awakening is.

Although I did a tremendous amount of work in collective awakening, and spent years facilitating discussion groups around the world that would catalyze this amazing experience, I eventually paused working in this way to focus on teaching meditation and mystical philosophy. There were two reasons for this. The first was because collective practice, sometimes known as we-space work, had gained some popularity and I felt I wanted to share a different approach that I needed to develop further. The other reason was because I felt that to enter into the mysterious spiritual union that I had experienced through collective awakening required being grounded in meditation with a cultivated ability to let go of our deep seated sense of identity.

For a number of years I worked with students supporting them to cultivate the profound inner freedom that I thought would create the spiritual ground for collective experiences of awakening to occur. Recently I have seen the miraculous emergence of a shared field of higher awareness occurring with increasing regularity among the people that I work with. Seeing this has inspired me to write this book.

In the pages that follow I expand on what I shared in *The Soul of a New Self*, by offering a more comprehensive guidebook to the practice of collective awakening. At the end of the book I introduce a dialog practice called *speaking from emptiness* which is designed to lead groups of sincere practitioners into profound heights of collective awakening. This book is meant to be used as a manual for practice. It offers both context and instruction for collective spiritual work. Specifically, that means guidance for attaining the profound depth of relaxed ease of being that is demanded of this work, as well as inquiries that loosen the grip of our familiar sense of self and make us available for a radical shift in identity.

It is my sincere hope that the insights and perspective you find here will inspire you to engage in dialogs that will reveal the deeper source of your being.

The world we live in is a co-creation, a manifestation of individual consciousness woven into a collective dream.

- Oriah Dreamer

JEFF CARREIRA

CHAPTER ONE

Collective Awakening and Meta Being

JEFF CARREIRA

IN RECENT DECADES, IN certain spiritually-minded circles, a phenomenon you could call collective awakening work, or is sometimes referred to as we-space work, has become popular. The idea of collective awakening is simple and compelling. Awakening or spiritual enlightenment, which is traditionally seen as a profound shift in the inner experience of an individual, now occurs within the shared space between people. An awakened field of consciousness is generated and all of the individuals that exist within that field experience the shift.

In our world in which so many problems stem from the inability of people to understand each other and get along, a shared field of enlightened awareness could be the answer to our collective prayers. This is exactly how it occurred to me when I first encountered this kind of spiritual work in a little known spiritual group that centered around a teacher who spoke passionately about the necessity of a collective awakening on Earth. The teacher claimed, and later I saw for myself, that among the people in this group, fields of awakened awareness could emerge in the space between them. What I later experienced was how collective awakening sweeps everyone up into an ecstatic state of higher consciousness that allows them to express themselves with deepened sensitivity, compassion, and wisdom.

The spiritual community that I lived in for twenty years was largely dedicated to developing the capacity to enter into these miraculous states at will. We wanted to be able to consistently come together and drop into the experience of what we called *a new being*. We worked together on this project relentlessly. During the first decade of my involvement the focus of the community was on creating the spiritual ground for collective awakening. We met in various configurations of dialog groups weekly, sometimes daily, during certain periods multiple times a day, and occasionally most of the day and late into the night. We also did many hours of individual spiritual practices including meditation, chanting, and prostrations. All of this was part of what we thought it would take to create fertile ground within each of us so that the miracle we wanted would occur.

As we saw it, the ground of collective awakening was dependent on the spiritual attainment of each individual. That meant that everyone needed to develop the capacity to act beyond their habitual sense of self.

We wanted to create the space for the birth of a new being, a new collective self. In order for a new self to be born through us, we needed to be able to leave our previous sense of self behind. All of our spiritual work was dedicated to generating inner freedom and a profound fluidity of identity. We needed to be able to act beyond our habitual sense of self, which meant we needed to be ready at any moment to let go of all of our ideas about who we were and become more than we thought was possible.

After nearly a decade of intensive and consistent spiritual work, I had the privilege of being part of a dramatic collective awakening. For a number of weeks a group of us burst into an experience of one-mind. That experience occurred during a two-month long retreat that included deep dialog discussions every evening. It was in these discussions that something profound started to be expressed by some of the members of the group. As I watched these individuals speak, I could see that they were speaking from the same place, their words were infused with the same sense of discovery, and they seemed to be half in this world and half in another.

During one of these meetings I experienced a shift in identity that brought me into unity with these other individuals, and in many ways has defined my life ever since. There came a moment when I was sitting in the group and felt deeply inspired to speak and started to think about what I would say. Then I stopped and rather than formulate my words, I simply allowed them to rise up and pass through my mouth.

I found myself speaking words before I knew what I was saying. It felt like something was speaking through me and describing my experience more precisely than I could. On the one hand it felt like I wasn't speaking at all, and yet the words being spoken were more mine than any I had ever spoken before. Our evening meetings continued and more and more of us entered this mysterious space of spoken surrender.

Once everyone in the group had let go into the awakening, a wild energy swirled through us and everyone spoke with clarity, conviction, and sensitivity, beyond anything they had experienced before. We all seemed to have gained access to what I would now call meta-being – a source of wisdom that engulfed us, emerged through us, and gave us access to possibilities beyond imagination. From that time forward I dedicated myself to discovering how to create the conditions that allow meta-being to be awakened and sustained between people. I've worked with people in different ways all over the world and I'm just as inspired by this work today as ever.

One of the things that I have learned about the process of collective awakening is that it depends on our willingness to liberate ourselves from our current sense of identity, so that we are available for something more. We have all learned to think of ourselves as an isolated individual – a separate thing in a universe filled with other things. Unless we see through the assumption of separate existence, at least to some degree, a new form of self cannot come forward.

As we let go of the false beliefs and assumptions that hold our current identity of separation and isolation in place, we discover that the person we think we are is largely a collection of stories about ourselves. Underneath all those stories, who we are is a mystery beyond comprehension. This is the great realization of emptiness that is talked about in many of the world's great spiritual traditions. It shows us that our current sense of self is not immutable – it can change. We can grow into a different sense of self – not just the same self with better qualities, but something dramatically different. We can become a different kind of human.

As we move further and further away from the stories we hold about ourselves and deepen into the direct experience of what is, we enter a profoundly free and fluid state of awareness. From here, we can discover together how to expand into a sense of self that reveals that underneath the familiar experience of isolation we are one being. This realization allows us to act with a degree of harmony and unification that is not available in a world dominated by the story of separation. I believe that when we engage together in the collective awakening of meta-being we are step-ping into the future of being human. It is impossible to experience this possibility without feeling that it is an essential part of the solution to all of humanity's problems.

In *The Soul of a New Self*, I describe in more detail the life-changing experience of collective awakening that I briefly described above, and I wrote extensively about what I saw as the philosophical and psychologi-cal ground required for it to emerge. In books like *The Art of Conscious Contentment*, *No Place But Home* and *The Experience of Luminous Absorption*, I've explored the practice of meditation, which has always been my primary individual practice. In this book, I offer an explanation of, and guidance for, orchestrating col-lective awakening. What you will discover here is how groups of people can prepare for, and engage in deep dialogs that catalyze the emergence of a shared experi-ence of being.

During the years that I was intensely focused on the work of collective awakening, I learned not to think of this work in terms of an experience of awakening that a number of people were experienc-ing together. Instead I thought of it as a new being, or a new self, that would emerge through a group of individuals and draw their minds into a higher shared mind. The notion of the emergence of a new being was a prominent idea of the theologian Paul Tillich, although I have come to prefer the term *meta-being* which I first heard in the writings of one of Tillich's students, the feminist theologian Mary Daly. She used the term in place of Tillich's *New Being* because she felt it didn't imply a break with the past but rather a more encompassing form of being that included what came before. This book is about my understanding of how we can awaken the mystery of meta-being between us.

As we move further and further away from the stories we hold about ourselves and deepen into the direct experience of what is, we enter a profoundly free and fluid state of awareness.

CHAPTER TWO

Varieties of Collective Awakening

BEFORE WE EXPLORE THE practices associated with collective awakening, we need to distinguish between a number of different ways that collective awakening can be thought of. I have already said that collective awakening is an awakening that emerges in the space between people. That space is sometimes called intersubjective because it exists between subjects. Whatever it is called, it is the place where we share a sense of reality. It includes shared values and assumptions, and any experiences of reality we hold in common. If we are at an exciting sports event, we might share a sense of jubilation with everyone in a stadium when our team scores a point. That experience exists in the intersubjective space between us.

The idea of collective consciousness has gained some attention for study in recent years. There have been both academic and popular books written about it. What generates so much excitement around the idea of collective consciousness is the observation of enhanced human capacities that seem to emerge in the space of shared consciousness. The metaphor that I like to use is a radio telescope created out of a satellite dish array. A single satellite dish can be used as a radio telescope that allows us to pick up radio waves emitted from deep space. How deeply into space a satellite dish can see depends on its size. The wider the dish, the deeper into space it can look.

The problem is that a single satellite dish can only be made so wide because of the amount of material that would be required to build an extremely large one. To create a satellite dish array you simply arrange many smaller satellite dishes in close proximity to each other spread out over a large area. What you find is that these dishes can be used in unison to effectively get the same power as you would get from a single dish of the same size as the total area covered. You could never build a single dish that is as big as the area you could cover with an array of smaller dishes.

Analogously, researchers in collective consciousness have found that groups of people working together under the right conditions experience increases in mental capacity. Artists who work together find their creativity is enhanced, and teams of scientists are often responsible for the most innovative new ideas. In the experience of collective awakening, my experience has been that in that shared field of higher consciousness, we gain access to greater insight, wisdom and love than we have on our own.

It has also been my experience that the term collective awakening is used in different ways, meaning different things in various contexts. What we will explore now is some of the ways the term may be used, and how we will be using it here.

When we say a person has had an awakening, we generally mean that they have had an inner revelation of higher awareness. In the case of a single individual this would be an experience that they had personally, independent of anyone else.

One way that the idea of collective awakening can be used is in describing a circumstance in which a group of people have the same revelation of higher awareness at the same time. In these cases the experiences are still fundamentally isolated events that individuals are having personally, but now it is happening to a number of individuals together at the same time. They are not sharing a single experience, but they can tell by speaking with one another that they are all having the same inner experience.

The experience of waking up this way with other people is very powerful because it provides instant validation of your experience. Having a spiritual experience when you are alone or the only one having it, is often confusing because you don't know if you can trust what's happening. When you experience the same awakening as the person next to you and you can talk about it together while it is happening, any doubt is diminished. We could call this *mutually reinforced inspiration*, and the growing sense of certainty that comes with this form of shared awakening fuels and accelerates the experience that everyone is having, and carries them to places beyond where they would likely go on their own.

So, the first form of collective awakening involves a number of people having a similar inner experience at the same time, in the same place. Another form, and in my opinion one that represents a deeper level of collective awakening, is where two or more people recognize oneness together. They experience non-separation and unity. They realize in an undeniable way that they are not separate. That they are one.

I have experienced this depth of spiritual union on numerous occasions, but there was one simple but powerful moment that I often remember. It occurred during the same retreat I wrote about earlier, but it happened while I was eating dinner with other participants. I was sitting across from someone, a man who was also a friend, and we happened to catch eyes. In that moment it was obvious that the being who was looking through his eyes at me, and the being that was looking through my eyes back at him, was the same being. There was one being, one source of awareness, emerging through two different bodies.

This level of collective awakening is more significant than two people having their own individual experiences at the same time, because in the shared experience of non-separation the connection between us is the source of revelation. We are not having two separate experiences of oneness, we could call this level of collective awakening *mutually recognized oneness* because I am not recognizing oneness in myself, I am seeing it in the other and they are seeing it in me. In the experience I just described, I knew beyond doubt that my friend was seeing what I was seeing, and I was seeing what he was seeing. The mutuality of the recognition was part of the experience itself. We did not need to talk about it to confirm it, we were experiencing oneness through each other. In experiences of mutual oneness, the sense of separation between people is transcended.

The Jewish theologian Martin Buber described encounters of this depth as I-Thou connections. In these connections we are not encountering another person as an object, we are encountering the living presence shining through the person and recognizing it to be the same as the living presence that animates ourselves. Seeing the living presence shining through another person reveals the universal source of life. The moment I saw the living presence in my friend's eyes on retreat was the first time that I had experienced this depth of oneness, and although I have experienced it numerous times since with individuals and among groups of people, I'm sure I will never forget this first sacred encounter.

One thing that I want to point out about the I-Thou encounter with living presence is that it is not ultimately about the personalities of the people involved. You don't have to like a person's personality, or have a particular chemistry with them personally in order to see the living presence shining through them. The spiritual union that occurs is ultimately oneness with the source of life. Of course, an experience of mutually recognized oneness must happen with another person or more people and will leave you deeply bonded. At the same time, you will know that you are connecting with something universal as well. I would like to note that this same experience can happen with other animal species and with any living thing. This book is focused on collective awakening between human beings, because there is something unique about the possibility of sharing this experience with a member of your own species, especially because it ignites a depth of unity that is generally unheard of in a world so riddled with mistrust.

There is another form of collective awakening that I have experienced, and again I see this as more significant and more profound than the previous two. In the experience of mutually recognized oneness that I just described we see oneness and unity in the connection between us. The next depth of collective awakening occurs when we don't just see oneness, we speak from it together. As I described earlier, my experience of this was speaking and hearing words coming out of my mouth, but feeling like they were not coming from me. They were coming from the oneness, from the higher beingness, aware and speaking through all of us. You don't just feel like you are recognizing oneness, but oneness is speaking through you. That higher being is speaking through you. It is verbalizing what it sees. We can call this level of collective awakening *mutually embodied oneness* and in the experience of it you feel like you are a channel for a higher self that is accessing the world through you.

When I first experienced this profound level of collective awakening, I knew that the higher meta-being that was speaking through me was also speaking through everyone else, and it was becoming aware of itself through us. At this level, the higher self is awakening to its own existence, more than you are awakening to it. You are an instrument of its being, and it has an existence beyond you. It is not that you feel separate from it, because you know that you are it and it is you. It is more than you, and you are that. You have discovered a higher being and recognized it to be yourself.

To summarize, I am introducing three distinct types or levels of collective awakening - *mutually reinforced inspiration*, *mutually recognized oneness*, and *mutually embodied oneness.* The first is simply two or more people having the same spiritual experience together at the same time and being able to share about it with each other. Each person is having an individual experience, but being able to share about it in real time dramatically enhances the experience through mutual reinforcement.

The next level is a shared realization of the oneness that occurs when two or more people recognize the living presence of universal being shining through each other. This is a mutual experience in the sense that the realization is not happening within the individuals, it is happening between them. The realization of oneness is happening inside of and because of the connection they share.

This third level occurs when we move beyond recognizing oneness together and discover how to allow the higher being to speak and recognize itself through us. At this point the awakening is no longer ours, it is the higher self that is waking up. If we continue to allow that meta-being to speak through us, we will see it growing, learning and discovering more about itself.

Now that we have outlined the basic elements of how I have experienced and come to understand collective awakening, we can go on in the chapters ahead to explore the contemplations, practices and methods that allow these mysterious shifts in consciousness to emerge between people.

JEFF CARREIRA

> *The higher self is awakening to its own existence, more than you are awakening to it. You are an instrument of its being, and it has an existence beyond you.*

CHAPTER THREE

Transformation and the Art of Self-Forgetting

I SEE THE PRACTICE of meditation as an important foundation for collective awakening and although I have written extensively in other books about it, again, here are a few things that describe the practice specifically in relation to its role in collective awakening.

In order for meta-being to emerge through us we must be available for it. To be available, we must be able to free ourselves of our own agendas and be ready to expand beyond who we think we are. So often in spiritual work a person will begin to experience a deeper, broader, and higher sense of self only to recoil from it at the exact moment when they need to relax into it. If we are clinging to who we think we are we will not be available to experience ourselves differently. The way I teach meditation allows you to develop the capacity to grow beyond your existing sense of self.

We have all learned to experience ourselves as an isolated individual who exists independent from other people and the rest of the world. We cannot expand into a collective identity if we are clinging to the identity of an isolated individual. Meditation is a practice that allows us to learn to be without an accompanying sense of identity. In other words, it is a practice of forgetting yourself. In this chapter I will introduce the practice of meditation as the art of self-forgetting, because this understanding clearly shows how meditation supports collective awakening.

Meditation can be thought of as the art of self-forgetting, which means literally the practice of forgetting yourself. To be explicitly clear, this doesn't mean you disappear, rather, you forget yourself. The emergence of collective awakening needs you to be present, so you're still here, but you also need to forget yourself so that you are free at the level of identity to become something else.

Meditation is only about disappearing to yourself. It is about being yourself without seeing yourself or knowing yourself. The goal of meditation is to let go of all self-consciousness so you are free, spontaneous and available to new possibilities. The goal is to forget yourself and just be whoever you are without self-reflecting. It is a flow state.

When we do something we love, for example skiing, biking, painting, writing, we often fall into what is called a flow state. In these states we continue doing what we are doing but we stop watching ourselves while we do it. All of our attention is focused on what we are doing, with no attention left to imagine ourselves doing it. These are the most fulfilling experiences we have, and we find that in these states of unselfconscious flow we experience peaks of efficiency, creativity, and performance.

In meditation we enter a flow state when we aren't doing anything except sitting still. We are in flow with being. When you meditate, simply close your eyes, breathing easily and naturally. Allow your body to come to rest and be comfortable and at peace. Just breathe and relax. Don't pay any attention to what your mind might be thinking. You should allow yourself to forget that you're meditating and forget where you are. Knowing that you're meditating, knowing where you are, and knowing what you're doing, are all utterly unnecessary. All you need to do is be. Just relax and blissfully forget what you're doing. Forget where you are. Forget who you are, Just rest in a perfect state of release and relief. Don't work at it. Don't be busy relaxing. Just be.

None of your ideas about who you are, where you are, or what you're doing matter. Allow yourself the luxury of forgetting everything. There is no need to worry about doing this correctly. You're just being, you're just here. There's no way to do it wrong.

If you manage to forget yourself, even for a few moments, you will feel how utterly wonderful it is. We spend so much energy watching ourselves, making decisions, and trying to control outcomes. All of this self-analysis and self-control is exhausting, but the habit is so deep it's very hard to break. It is very difficult for us to let go and just be.

In the Hindu tradition they say that we all get a taste of deep self-forgetting every night when we fall asleep. As we relax, get comfortable and let go of consciousness, we do not disappear, we forget ourselves. It is possible to let your mind and body fall asleep while you remain awake. I have watched myself fall asleep, and then remained awake while my mind and body continued to sleep. These have been among the most extraordinary things I've ever experienced. When it happens, my breathing becomes automatic, my body grows rigid beyond my control, my mind moves in and out of dream states, by every indication I am asleep, except I am awake watching it all happen. These experiences have left me personally certain that I am a free-floating conscious awareness that is able to pass through this mind and body yet exists beyond each of them.

When we see that we are the consciousness that passes through our human form, we simultaneously realize that this same consciousness could just as easily pass through a different form. This experience of profound freedom from form is a crucial realization on the path to collective awakening. I don't want this to sound like the recognition of free floating awareness diminishes the significance of our minds or bodies, any more than the emergence of a butterfly diminishes the existence of the caterpillar that it was. Our human form is beautiful, profound, sacred and should be honored. We are privileged to have been born as a human being and at the same time, our current form is not the limit of what is possible for us.

When we practice the art of self-forgetting, or unknowing as it has been called in some Christian literature, we give up control and let go of our self-awareness. We forget where we are, who we are, and what we're doing. The interesting question that arises when we do this is, *who are we when we forget ourselves?* Since you don't remember, you could be anyone. Developing the capacity to forget yourself in the way that we're speaking about is an essential part of the path of spiritual transformation, because when you're no longer holding on to the person you think you are, you are available to be someone else, you're available to transform. We can't hold on to who we are and become someone else at the same time.

In order for the meta-being of collective awakening to occur we must participate. The higher order of meta-being is dependent on our presence, but it also needs us to get out of the way. It needs us to be present and available. We become available for this transformation by forgetting ourselves. If we find a way to forget who we are, we will be ready to be inhabited by a dramatically different way of being human.

The mystery of collective awakening that we are exploring in this book is fundamentally a transformation of the sense of self. It is a shift in identity. Can we come together and forget who we are long enough to be engulfed by a unifying vision of oneness, and surrender deeply enough to allow that oneness to speak and act through us. This book is an invitation to an awakening that we can have together to bring a higher order of beingness to life between us. The potential of a collectively awakened individuality is the birth of a higher order of love and wisdom in the world. Now it is time to explore how we can work together to do this.

The emergence of collective awakening needs you to be present, so you're still here, but you also need to forget yourself so that you are free at the level of identity to become something else.

CHAPTER FOUR:

Attunement and Availability

JEFF CARREIRA

A CRUCIAL SKILL IN practices of collective awakening is what I call attunement, which is essentially a kind of deep listening. It is more than just hearing with your ears and understanding with your mind. It is a recalibration of your perspective through a form of deep listening that happens throughout your being. What you are doing is listening to what someone is saying and tuning in to the way they are perceiving. In the current context of collective awakening that means tuning into the energy of awakening in the words that are being spoken.

A good metaphor to use for this process is a tuning fork. The way you use a tuning fork is by striking it so that it vibrates with the energy of a particular musical note. You can then use that vibration as a point of reference when tuning an instrument. When an instrument is playing the same note as the tuning fork you will hear it and know it is in tune. This is a good analogy to spiritual attunement. You know you are attuned to the speaker when what they say resonates with you so deeply that it feels they could easily be your words coming out of their mouth. When you are in spiritual attunement with someone it feels like they are reading your mind. You find that you could finish every sentence they say and anticipate what they will say next. You are in tune with them and it feels like you have the same mind. This is the simplest way to understand the experience of mutually embodied oneness.

This process of attuning is what allows us to be available to collective awakening. In dialog or even in silence, the only thing that you need to be concerned with is tuning into the energy of awakening together. When two or more people are tuned into each other this way, they are available to be swept up in a mutual experience of oneness. Attunement is what makes the experience of mutually embodied oneness possible. The more attuned we are together the more available we are to give birth to a higher order of being. In any group of people where everyone is available for this breakthrough, it will happen. This higher order consciousness wants to emerge here on Earth. It will appear through any opening it is given. It simply needs a group of two or more people who are open to it. The awakening will happen all by itself, all we have to do is be ready for it.

One of the ways that we remain unavailable is by insisting on understanding everything before we relax. Our minds will always be full of considerations. They want to know how this works and if it is safe. The mind will continuously generate a string of questions and then insist that they must be answered before we can let go. Getting overly involved with these questions amounts to putting on the brakes and stopping the process. And yes, this is a tricky business. You can't be naive. You must determine that the process you are about to engage with works and is safe, but that can only be determined to a certain degree. Once you feel reasonably ready, you have to let go. To the mind it will never feel reasonable, there will always be more questions to answer first. Remember, there will never be complete certainty, you need to take the leap anyway.

Taking the leap means tuning into the people around you, letting yourself see things the same way they do, and then relaxing to a profound degree. Of course the depth of trust that must exist between people to make this possible is itself unusual. Developing that depth of trust is why it took many years of doing spiritual practice together in a residential community before this miracle started to emerge between us. Before then there was simply not enough trust established in the group to allow for the depth of relaxation required when we were together.

The relaxation needed for collective awakening to occur is a deep relaxation of our conscious minds and our bodies, but it is more than that. We must relax our unconscious mind as well. That means relaxing our unconscious defenses and reactive tendencies too. These unconscious mechanisms will keep us from being swept up beyond our familiar sense of self, reflexively reasserting our old identity when its dominance feels threatened. Even if we consciously want to transform, our unconscious tendencies will keep us anchored in the familiar sense of who we are. This will only work if we are able to abide in a profound depth of relaxation and override our reactive inner tendencies. Yes, overriding your unconscious defense mechanisms is dangerous. You need to be reasonably certain that you are in a trustworthy situation before you begin. And as I just said, it will never be possible to be completely certain and so at some point you are going to need to decide you are ready.

Making yourself available means becoming consciously vulnerable. That means trusting and letting go. You can't relax without trust. So what allows us to become more available to the process of attuning is trusting more and more and more. That means trusting yourself first of all, trusting the people you are working with, and trusting the process of collective awakening. As you trust more, you will relax more, as you relax more, the sense of self-concern falls away and you are able to forget yourself. As you forget yourself, you become available to be moved by spiritual energies and swept up into the miracle of mutually embodied oneness.

> *Making yourself available means becoming consciously vulnerable. That means trusting and letting go. You can't relax without trust. So what allows us to become more available to the process of attuning is trusting more and more and more.*

CHAPTER FIVE

Intersubjectivity

THE WORD INTERSUBJECTIVITY REFERS to the space of shared awareness between us. Subjective awareness is the awareness of our own interior space, intersubjective awareness is the awareness of our shared interior space, or what has sometimes been more popularly known as we-space. I've done a great deal of work with others focused on this shared inner space. I have experienced dramatic, powerful and very positive results, and I have seen it go wrong. When working with intersubjectivity I want to work in the same way I work with meditation, as simply and straightforwardly as possible. Which to me means first of all, not making too big a deal out of the idea of intersubjectivity or collective we-space. The reason I want to avoid too much fanfare around it is because the experience we're having all the time is always already happening in an intersubjective we-space. We are never actually isolated even if the habitual ways of thinking of the current paradigm overwhelmingly tend to make us think of ourselves that way.

The consciousness that we experience is always a combination of an individual unique perspective that belongs to you personally and a generally invisible background consciousness full of assumptions, attitudes, ideas and feelings that are not yours. This background of understanding comes from the intersubjective spaces of family, friends, co-workers, nationalities and cultures. We have all been enculturated to relate to our inner space as if it belongs only to us. We are taught that when we look inside, we are looking at a different inner world than the person next to us is when they look inside. It is analogous to living in my own house. When I go inside my house it has its own interior. I don't walk into my house and end up in yours. The analogy of a house appears to be deeply interconnected with our sense of self. So much so in fact, that it is often said that houses that appear in our dreams are representations of ourselves.

We are conditioned to think about ourselves the way we think about a house, my house leads to my interior and yours has its own interior. In doing the work of collective awakening a different analogy will serve us better by shaping an understanding of ourselves that leaves us more available to the miracle. What if when I look inside and you look inside, we're looking at the same inside? What if the inner space of consciousness was not like the inside of the house, but the outside world? Maybe when I look inside it is like opening the door to my house and looking out at the world - the inner world. Maybe there are not many different insides but only one.

When I look out of my door at the world and you look out of yours, we're looking at the same world from two different places. Maybe the inner world of consciousness is the same. When I look inside myself and you look inside yourself, we are looking at the same interior world from two different places.

In the world of we-space work, I feel that sometimes people make the idea of intersubjectivity seem too out of the ordinary and unusual, when in fact it is largely an overlooked aspect of our everyday experience. Making the idea of intersubjectivity alien to our familiar experience makes it more difficult to attain. When we realize that the collective awakening we are seeking has more to do with turning our attention to a largely overlooked part of our normal experience, it makes it attainable. I also think that it is more accurate. I don't think collective awakening is something new, it is an enhancement of something that is already a part of us. That being said, it is not just a small tweak either. It is a major reorientation to the experience you're already having.

I have already described the metaphor of a radio telescope dish array, but I want to return to it now to help us gain a better sense of the magnitude of the reorientation that we're talking about, and the spiritual potential of it. The largest radio telescope in the world is located in southwestern China and measures five hundred meters wide. That is wider than five American football fields. Can you imagine how difficult and expensive it is to build a structure that large? You might be wondering why they make radio telescopes so big, the answer is because the wider the dish the greater the dish's capacity to pick up the very weak signals of cosmic waves coming from deep space. A wider dish can pick up weaker cosmic signals and look deeper into space.

The massive radio telescope in China is the largest radio telescope in the world, but it is not the most powerful. The Very Large Array (VLA) located in New Mexico in the United States consists of twenty-seven separate dishes measuring twenty-five meters across. When these dishes are used together as one, they have an effective diameter of twenty-two miles. Currently this constitutes the most powerful radio telescope on Earth.

An array of radio telescopes allows us to look much more deeply into space. No single radio telescope that was twenty-two miles wide could possibly be built. Yet an array of just twenty-seven dishes measuring only twenty-five meters has the same power. The effect of collective awakening is similar. Remember that when we look inside ourselves we are looking into the depths of inner space in the same way that a telescope looks into the night sky above. Any one of us on our own can only look so deep, but when we come together bound into the mysterious unity of collective awakening, we can see much further. A group of people who have attuned their hearts, minds, and souls are like a radio telescope array of inner space. Together we can hear murmurings of spirit so faint that no individual could ever hear. This is the great spiritual value of collective awakening; it multiplies our spiritual sensitivity. Many years of collective spiritual practice have confirmed this for me. When we attune together we can reach further into the depths of our inner spirit and uncover the riches of insight, wisdom and guidance that are found there.

This is how I suggest we think about collective work together. As we attune, as we become available, as we relax together - we begin to generate a field of awakening that is collectively held by all of us. And that field is able to perceive more deeply into the mystery of being than any individual could, and we all have the benefit of being part of that shared field.

We all benefit from being in that shared field, and we all have the responsibility of doing our part to help maintain it, which by now you've probably realized has to do with giving everything you can to tune in, open, trust, be available and relax.

"

As we attune, as we become available, as we relax together - we begin to generate a field of awakening that is collectively held by all of us. And that field is able to perceive more deeply into the mystery of being than any individual could, and we all have the benefit of being part of that shared field.

CHAPTER SIX

Creative Union and the Living Universe

My book *THE SOUL of a New Self,* begins with a discussion of the French paleontologist and evolutionary spiritual pioneer, Peirre Teilhard de Chardin. In his spiritual writing he speaks about what he calls the process of creative union through which new beings come into existence. I find his idea fascinating and inspiring. He describes how a new being begins as a soul which is nothing more than an energetic field. The soul is an organizing principle that resonates at a particular frequency and attracts things of the same frequency to itself. It's a very beautiful metaphor. The soul energy gathers its body and builds its mental or material existence around itself. Teilhard saw this process of creative union as the fundamental process of birth that occurs at all levels of existence. New human babies form this way and so do new ideas, fears and aspirations.

As we attune to the energy and frequency of awakening together, we are being gathered around a soul that wants to exist. There is a new way of being, a meta-being, that wants to be born and it is drawing us together. At its inception that possibility only exists as an energetic attractor that acts like a tractor beam from science fiction stories that pull on any elements that resonate at the same energy. The soul signal is very faint initially and very few people are sensitive enough to pick it up, but as more of us attune to it, the signal grows in strength and becomes available to more people. When we attune together we are collectively aligning our energy in a particular way with perspectives and recognitions that belong to a new way of being human. When enough of us come together, something ignites, and that new possibility becomes independently stable.

Let's think a little more about how the amplification of the soul signal happens. We can use the concept of resonance from physics to create a picture of what is happening. When two waves of the same frequency overlap, the crests and troughs of the waves combine to create a new wave. How much the amplitude of the wave increases through this combination depends on how well the crests and troughs of the waves match up. If the waves are perfectly in phase the crest peaks of one wave will coincide with those of the other. These two waves are said to be in resonance and the resultant wave will have twice the amplitude of the two original ones. This is how energy waves combine to increase in amplitude and power.

The phenomenon of resonance was dramatically illustrated when the Tacoma Narrows Bridge collapsed on November 7th, 1940. On a day of gusty forty mile per hour winds in Washington State, the bridge began to sway with a twisting motion. It just so happened that the length of the bridge and the timing and speed of the wind came into resonance amplifying the effect of the wind on the bridge. Over a short span of time the massive structure of the bridge twisted itself apart and crumbled into the river below. When energetic vibrations come into resonance they increase in power. I offer the example of the Tacoma Narrows Bridge as a metaphorical example to illustrate what happens when our spiritual energies on a psychic level come into resonance. The result of the increased psychic power does not tear things apart, but attracts more people who can tune into the same frequency.

If you're reading this book, I'm confident that you've already started to feel the compulsion to come together with others in a higher vibration. You've probably also intuited that in this way you could support the birth of a new way of being. I believe that the reason that collective spiritual work has increased in popularity is because more people are sensing the soul energy of the meta-being. I don't know what karmic circumstances allow some people to feel drawn to that energy and not others, but I do know that once it comes to life in you, you start spiritually vibrating at that frequency and attracting others to you. The signal will start very weak, maybe only strong enough to attract you to read this book, but as you continue the work it will get stronger. The most important thing is that you are vibrating with that energy now and calling things into your life that will support it to grow. I imagine that you have already noticed how people are drawn into your life for mysterious reasons that neither of you can fully understand. Perhaps this is because you are both being called to participate in the birth of a higher order of being.

For the past few years I felt reluctant to teach collective awakening. One of the reasons for that is because the way it is often approached feels overly anthropocentric. In other words, this type of spiritual work tends to be centered on human intersubjectivity and I feel that it must be extended beyond the human world in order for us to realize the full potential of what's being revealed. The awakening that we are talking about is an awakening that happens in the shared inner space between people, but we don't want to assume that space is limited to humans, to what we commonly think of as feelings, emotions and ideas.

The term intersubjectivity, which refers to the inner space between us, was coined by the German philosopher Edward Husserl, who is the founder of the discipline of phenomenology. Husserl talked about intersubjectivity as the shared interior space in which the entire world arises. He recognized that the world we live in is experiential by nature. We have been taught to believe that we are experiencing a material world, but all we have access to is an experiential world. From this perspective we live in a subjective experience of reality, a phenomenal world. What makes the phenomenal world remain stable is the fact that it is not dependent on only one subjective experience, it is held together collectively as a shared intersubjective experience. We are all holding an experience of reality together and then we live in that reality. This view is profound, but it still privileges human consciousness. We are still the species holding reality together.

I believe we're always having an intersubjective experience, even when we're alone. In fact, I believe that the world we live in is more of an intersubjective experience than it is a physical place. The sense of an outside solid objective reality is more of a shared experience held in place by our collective beliefs and assumptions than it is an objective outer world. Doing intersubjective, we-space, spiritual work is challenging in part because we are always experiencing an intersubjective reality. Teaching intersubjectivity is a little like teaching a fish about the existence of water. Fish have always lived in water and it's very difficult to point out something that has always existed everywhere. Spend a little time contemplating the possibility that all of this world is not an independently objective place that would continue to exist even if all the living beings in it were removed. Instead Imagine that the world is actually an intersubjective experience that we are all holding together.

Let's expand this conversation beyond human intersubjectivity, because I don't believe that reality is held only in human consciousness. I believe that reality is multi-dimensional and there are other conscious beings and other forms of consciousness throughout it. The work we are exploring in this book is spiritual work designed for human beings because that is the form we happen to be in, but the experience of collective awakening can take us far beyond our current sense of being human and ultimately beyond any sense of separation at all. When we come together with others and see that the consciousness that animates all of us is coming from the same source, we recognize that we are all a part of a universe that is a single conscious entity.

The most exciting potential of collective or intersubjective awakening is that it can reveal, amplify and reinforce the mystical revelation that everything is part of a living whole. My experience has shown me that when we open to oneness together, we discover that everything that exists is part of a harmonious union of life. Everything is acting and communicating together as one, and that means that we are constantly receiving messages through the things and circumstances around us. Every aspect of the world can communicate with us, and the more open we are, the more obvious this is. I have had questions answered by staring at a tree or sitting and listening to the sound of a river flowing by. I believe that this is what mystics throughout history have talked about as communion with the divine.

This is what the revelation of collective awakening can lead to. You don't need to take what I am saying at face value. This book gives you a few different perspectives and metaphors to work with. The way to work with them is not to analyze them to determine if they are accurate or correct, but instead to find ideas that you resonate with, ones that you recognize to be true yourself, and give your attention to those. Find places in this text that you authentically feel energetically in touch with. Notice the inner sense of excitement that vibrates around these ideas. Then rest in that energy and give more of your attention to it. As you do, you'll be pulled toward the energetic source of that vibration and you will shine brighter at that frequency. Ideas, things, circumstances and people will mysteriously find their way to you. You will hear the perfect phrase when you need it, the right person will walk into your life, or you'll find the right book showing up in your hand. I have experienced this type of resonance. It feels like you are working in harmony with existence and are being supported in everything you do.

I believe that if we only see the potential of collective awakening as an experience that exists between people, we will not unleash the full power of that spiritual union. Collective awakening is bigger than our personal awakening, and it is bigger than any group experience. Collective awakening is about the awakening of the conscious source of the universe. It is about the awakening of life itself.

"

*As we attune to the energy and
frequency of awakening together,
we are being gathered around a soul
that wants to exist. There is a new
way of being, a meta-being, that
wants to be born and it is drawing
us together.*

CHAPTER SEVEN

A New Self in Oneness

JEFF CARREIRA

IN THE THIRD CHAPTER of this book we spoke about the critical role of self-forgetting in the process of collective awakening. The reason for that is because in order for us to be available for collective awakening we must be ready to expand beyond the limits of who we think we are. We all have a strongly established sense of self. And when I say this I mean a strong sense that I am Jeff. Jeff is a person who was born on my birthday, has lived my life, has my memories, abides in this body, knows and feels what I know and feel. I am Jeff. Think about this for yourself. You have been conditioned to assume that your name refers to a person and you are that person. Many of us have had spiritual experiences that have convinced us that we are more than the collection of things that our name points to. We have recognized the unfathomable mystery behind our being, but the habit of thinking of ourselves as the person who has our name is stubbornly persistent. In that all important moment when the invitation to let go of who we are and allow a higher collective self to come through arrives, we must not hesitate. If we recoil in uncertainty at that delicate moment, we will pull back into our habitual sense of self and the higher possibility will pass by.

We have learned to see ourselves as human and we have learned to understand what it means to be human in a very particular way. When we use the word human being, we think of an organism with a body. We think of a person with two arms and two legs. We think of a physical body. The way we have been conditioned to think means that being a human being and having a human body are assumed to go together. To move forward on the path of collective awakening we must learn to decouple the idea of the sense of self being attached to any form of physical or even mystical body. If we can only imagine a being as having some form of body, it will be impossible for us to let go deeply enough to encounter another form of being all together.

Our sense of self is very tied to our material body. We all recognize that our body is not the limit of who we are. We say that we have a hand, or an arm, or a foot. Statements like these reinforce the sense that I possess a body, but am more than that. Still our sense of self is largely rooted in the physical form. That means that when we talk about one universal being, we are most likely to start imagining the universe as some kind of a body that holds consciousness.

When we talk about a higher order of being speaking through everyone during a collective awakening, we likely imagine a ghostly other-dimensional figure speaking through us.

The most important preparation for collective awakening is loosening the grip that our familiar sense of self has on our perception of reality. We see reality through the lens of our sense of self. Being available for the radical shift into meta-being requires us to be open to a breathtaking new perception of reality. We are so habituated to experience a sense of self that is intimately tied to our physical bodies that it can be difficult to imagine any other possibility. I attended a philosophy conference some years ago in which I heard a speaker offer a different understanding of the sense of self. I found the talk deeply compelling and very helpful in terms of providing an alternative to imagine.

The speaker asked us to consider the possibility that our sense of self was not based solely on our physical lifetime and our personal history, but instead was based on the effects we have in the world. That would mean that if we wrote a book our sense of self would extend to include all of the times people read or thought about the book, or any of the ways they acted differently as a result. If we introduced two people who eventually got married, our sense of self would live in that union. If our actions resulted in someone being happy or upset our sense of self would live in that feeling. Our self would extend well beyond the immediate reach of our body and might continue long after our body had ceased to function.

Imagine if your psyche had been shaped by this conception of self so that you actually felt yourself in the effects you had. You felt yourself in your friends' marriage, or in the person reading your book. You would no longer feel like a localized self, rooted in the immediate experience of embodiment. You would be spread out over space and time and exist in the continuous ripple of consequences that stemmed from your life. Rather than a physical body, you would have a consequential body. Take a moment to imagine what this sense of self would feel like. I do not mean to imply that this is the sense of self you should adopt. I offer it only as an example of something different. The goal here is not to adopt any particular new sense of self. The goal is simply to open to the fact that our familiar sense of self is not the only possible sense of self.

It is important to remember that collective awakening is not just a spiritual experience that a number of people have together. Collective awakening in the form of mutually embodied oneness is an awakening of a higher order of being. It is not a thing in the familiar sense, but it is a form of being. We are trained to think of ourselves as a physical thing and so we assume that any other being will be some similar kind of thing. As we open to the possibility of collective awakening we must embrace a very different sense of self. We are not just a physical thing that has been given a name. We are not just a person with a history that started on our birthday and will end when our body dies. We are a being, which is more like a way of being, or a beingness. We are not the only kind of being in existence. There are other ways to be. The mystery of collective awakening is an awakening to another way of being. If we surrender to this possibility we will see new thoughts, new feelings, new perceptions and new realities emerging through us. We will become a different kind of human being, in the sense that we will bring a new way of being to life in the world.

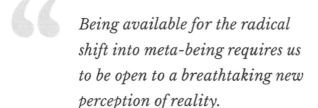

Being available for the radical shift into meta-being requires us to be open to a breathtaking new perception of reality.

CHAPTER EIGHT

Beyond the Familiar Self

I HAVE SHARED A great detail in this book about the importance of loosening the grip that our familiar sense of self has over our psyche. Now I will offer instructions for two contemplations that can help release you from the hold of your familiar sense of self. Please read through to the end of this chapter and then sit and follow the guidance it offers for contemplation. Go as deeply into these contemplations as you can, and if you are actively engaged in any intersubjective spiritual work, repeat them periodically.

As we've discussed at length, we are deeply conditioned by a particular sense of self that is associated with the experience of embodiment. Our sense of self is that of an isolated individual that feels localized in space so I feel like I exist over here in my body, not over there in yours, and you feel like you exist over there in your body and not here in mine. You can do the following interesting experiment in a group or if you are alone, you can simply imagine yourself doing it.

Sit in a circle and have everyone touch the shoulders of the people on either side of them. Notice that you can see the shoulders of everyone present, but you can only feel the shoulders that are being touched by the people sitting next to you. The shoulders you can feel are the ones you call yours, the ones that you can see but cannot feel belong to someone else. Now shift your consciousness so that you see all of the shoulders as yours and imagine that you are feeling all of the shoulders that are being touched in the circle. What you notice as you sit in this contemplation is that the way you define what is yours and what is not, is more arbitrary than you might initially think. The shoulders that I can see and feel are mine, the ones that I can see but can't feel are someone else's. Why can't the shoulders that I only see also be mine? Who decided that the sensation of physical contact is what determines who I am and who I am not?

We can take this contemplation a step further by asking ourselves how our perception might have evolved differently if we lived in a culture which believed that everyone you can see is part of you. Maybe in that case our sense of self would be defined by our visual field rather than physical sensation. Or maybe, our physical sense of touch would extend and we would actually feel the contact of all the shoulders we saw being touched. Our nervous system has been conditioned to perceive reality in accordance with the way we believe reality is. We believe that we are a particular kind of being and so we experience the world as if we are that. If we change the way we see ourselves we will also change the way we experience reality.

Collective awakening is an opportunity to awaken with other people in a shared recognition that we are all part of the same conscious awareness. If we spend time among others within whom this reality is alive, we will gain increasing depths of access to the luminous source that is animating our mind and body. If we continue to deepen our collective practice, our identity will shift so that we increasingly perceive ourselves to be that living source. The overarching point is that we won't be able to follow the transformative process to a shift in vision that extreme, until we leave our familiar sense of self behind.

Another contemplation that can help free ourselves from our ordinary sense of self is to think of collective awakening as a new experience of being human. To begin, take a few minutes to pay attention to your experience. Maybe you are sitting in a chair holding this book. Allow all of the richness of the experience of being you to come to life. Look at the room around you. Hear the sounds from outside the window. Feel the sensations in your body. Let it all in. So much of the time we are focused on a small portion of our experience. In this exercise open up to as much of your experience as you can.

Once you have opened to the full experience of the moment, notice if you imagine yourself to be the person experiencing it. We conventionally talk about 'our' experience, and so we naturally think of ourself as the person having the experience. When we talk about collective awakening we inevitably think of it as a new experience that we will have. This kind of thinking will not allow for the most profound possibilities of collective awakening to emerge. Rather than thinking about us having a new experience, I suggest that we think about a new experience of being human. This may sound like merely word play, but I can assure you that it's not. The shift I'm about to describe is simple but subtle, so go slow and think carefully.

Take another moment to pay attention to the experience you are having. Naturally your attention turns toward all of the different things that you are experiencing, but I also want you to include your experience of being the one who is experiencing those things. We don't just experience things, we also experience ourselves experiencing them. All of that taken together, everything we are experiencing and our experience of being the one experiencing it, is the experience of being human. The experience of being human that exists on this planet at this time, is the experience of perceiving all the different kinds of things we all tend to, while simultaneously feeling ourselves to be the one perceiving it all. I want you to let go of any assumption that you are the person having your experience, and simply see it all as the experience of being human.

When the experience of being human changes, familiar things will be perceived differently and entirely new things will appear in perception, but that is not all. We expect to perceive things differently after a shift in vision, what we seemingly are never ready for is that we are different too. After a dramatic shift, we do not feel like the same person we were. There may still be a sense of someone having that experience, but we cannot recognize that person as being us, and we might not even be able to recognize them as being human. When radical spiritual transformation happens, we are almost never ready to be dramatically different. We might be ready for the world to change, we might even be ready for aspects of ourselves to change, but are we ready to be a different kind of being in the middle of it all?

Please think about what this implies. Imagine yourself going through a transformative process so profound that you don't recognize yourself as being human anymore. Will you be able to relax into that depth of change? Or will you recoil and snap back into your familiar self? If you snap back, the transformation will instantaneously become a memory of something that you won't even be sure really happened. Unfortunately that is the fate of many transformations, because we consciously or unconsciously pull away from them and when we do they dissipate. In an instant we have returned to our familiar sense of self and the incomprehensible transformation we had just experienced is now something we only remember.

Collective awakening, like all deep spiritual transformations, is not something that happens to you. It is not your awakening. It is the awakening of a new way of being. A new way of being includes entirely new perceptions of familiar things, the appearance of totally new things to perceive, and a completely different sense of who or whatever is perceiving it all. If we are pursuing collective awakening, we need to be prepared for a change this vast. We need to be ready for a different way of being.

.

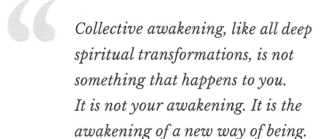

Collective awakening, like all deep spiritual transformations, is not something that happens to you. It is not your awakening. It is the awakening of a new way of being.

CHAPTER NINE

Being Deeply Relaxed

ONE OF THE THINGS that can get in the way of intersubjective spiritual work is when the idea of intersubjectivity is seen as a particular kind of experience. As we explored in chapter six, I see all of our experiences, from the most ordinary to the most extraordinary, as intersubjective. Sometimes intersubjective or we-space forms of spiritual work overidentify intersubjectivity with a particular experience, leaving the impression that the rest of our experience is not intersubjective. If we approach collective awakening this way we will almost certainly be trying to generate a specific feeling, usually an intense feeling of emotional connection, which is a beautiful experience to have, but is not in my opinion, more intersubjective than any other experience.

The miracle of intersubjective awakening lies in the fact that it is already here and we are already having it. We are not pursuing an experience that is different from the one we're having now. The underlying unity that is revealed in collective awakening is not found in a different experience; it is found in a subtle shift in how we relate to the experience we're already having. We can get trapped in spiritual work, whether it's individual or collective, when it overemphasizes the pursuit of new and better experiences. Collective awakening is not something we pursue, we can't hunt it down. It is already here right in front of us. If we are chasing after it, we will miss it. What we need to do is learn to relax more deeply into what is already here. That is why I see the practice of deep relaxation as essential preparation for this work.

Meditation has always been a foundational spiritual practice for me. In chapter three we explored meditation as the art of self-forgetting. From this perspective, meditation allows us to forget who we are, and be available to become someone else. Meditation can also be seen simply as the practice of relaxation. When I say this I do not mean that it is a practice of relaxing, it is the practice of sitting and being totally relaxed. Relaxing is an activity, being relaxed is not. Meditation is not an activity. This may sound simple, but most people find that it is more difficult than it sounds, and it tends to get more difficult the longer we meditate.

It is important to realize that relaxed is what we are when we don't do something else. Being relaxed is not something you do, it is already present as soon as you are not doing anything. Our habit of being occupied by doing, is so strong that we think we have a hard time relaxing, but being relaxed is effortless. It is not hard to relax, it is hard to stop doing things. If we want to experience the mystery of collective awakening we must develop a profound capacity to be relaxed, because when intersubjective consciousness opens we will be tempted to do something, but anything we do will reestablish the prominence of the individual isolated sense of self and shut down the opening. At that critical moment our most deeply ingrained instincts will tell us to do something. Any action we take will derail the delicate process that has begun, even if it is only the simple movement to try to understand what is happening.

In order to remain relaxed as we are swept away into the unknown, we need to have developed a deep habit of being relaxed. As you will see more directly in the chapters ahead, our ability to disengage from all activity becomes the ground that we rest in during intersubjective practices. Our capacity to be disengaged and deeply relaxed can be developed through the practice of meditation, and the instructions for meditation in this context can be most simply stated as "sit and be relaxed".

When we do this practice we release habitual patterns of engagement at many different levels, conscious and unconscious. The first and most obvious level is physical. We want to learn to be relaxed in our bodies and let go of all muscular tension. Some of this tension is obvious, like shaking your foot or clenching your teeth, but as we pursue this practice we will begin to find that unconscious tensions, places that were tight without our being aware that they were, will also release. We usually don't recognize this depth of tension until it actually lets go. You might be sitting seemingly relaxed and suddenly something lets go. Some unconscious tension is released. It might be experienced as an immediate feeling of relief, but it can also be experienced as pain or discomfort. When we practice the meditation of being relaxed we simply allow our bodies to unwind their inner tensions, moving into deeper and deeper rest.

Most of us find the idea of being relaxed very attractive, but the depth of relaxation that we are talking about can be frightening. Inevitably you come to a place in yourself where you can't imagine being more relaxed than you are. It often feels like something bad will happen if you let go any more. Bursts of fear, sometimes bordering on panic, can arise. You're afraid you will fall over, or fall asleep, or lose control in a dangerous way. At some point we're simply afraid to give up that much control, but if we are interested in the radical shift into intersubjective being, we need to give up control. In the end being relaxed means giving up control.

The practice of meditation begins by being relaxed in the body, then in the mind, but the most profound relaxation is not about the body or the mind; it is about you. In the end being relaxed is more than your body and mind being relaxed, it is about you being relaxed no matter what your mind and body are doing. At this point we discover that we can be completely relaxed in relation to everything, including the existence of tension in our mind and body. I have written in detail in other books about meditation and the profound depths of relaxation you can realize through it. I consider the ability to be relaxed to be a crucial component of the process of collective awakening and I believe that maintaining a strong practice of meditation must go hand in hand with any type of collective spiritual work.

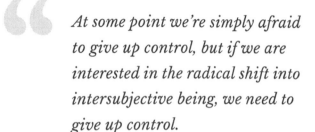

At some point we're simply afraid to give up control, but if we are interested in the radical shift into intersubjective being, we need to give up control.

CHAPTER TEN

The Necessity of Community

WE CAN'T THINK DEEPLY enough about how profoundly we are predisposed to assume that we are somebody. The idea that I am a person with a name is constantly being reinforced. We meet someone and they ask, who are you? and I respond, I am Jeff. The American philosopher John Dewey, who was also an early pioneer of psychology, offered some keen insights about how our sense of self develops. He points out that when we think about a baby being born, we assume that someone is born. We assume that the person who was born on your birthday gradually learned who they were. We were born and then we learned that we had a name and gradually we learned about ourselves. We learned that we are a particular person. In my case, I learned that I'm a boy whose name is Jeff, who is good at some things, and not so good at others. We learn more and more about the person that we are throughout our childhood.

Dewey suggested that maybe there is no self that's born on your birthday, maybe you are just a mind and body - a biological machine - at birth. That machine is equipped with a nervous system that responds to pleasure and pain, and learns behaviors. When babies are born, the adults around them think of them as a person with a name. They repeat that name over and over again until the baby starts to respond to it and the adults respond with joy that the baby experiences as pleasure. Soon the baby is consistently responding to the sound of their name. We think they have learned, but they have not learned their name, they have simply developed the habit of responding to the sound of their name. They don't know what it means. A habit of responding to the sound of our name has formed and everyone who responds positively when the baby reacts to the sound of their name is reinforcing the habit. The baby doesn't know its name, it has simply developed a habit of reacting to it. As the baby grows through childhood new habits are reinforced. The child develops habits of thinking and speaking about itself in certain ways. These ways are introduced by circumstances and other people and reinforced until the habits are strong. We develop habits of thinking of ourselves as smart or not, as industrious or lazy, as athletic or awkward. As habitual ways of thinking and speaking about ourselves are reinforced, they form our identity and we tend to act in ways that conform to them.

This gives us another way to think about the sense of self. Unlike what we discussed in chapter seven, where we introduced the possibility that the sense of self could be seen as the effects that we are having, we now imagine that the sense of self is a set of habitual ways of thinking, speaking and acting. Our sense of self is a collection of habits, but where are these habits located? Certainly they are located in our own minds and bodies, but they are also located in the people who know us. In fact, our sense of self actually begins in the minds of others. We are somebody to the people around us long before we feel like somebody to ourselves.

In relation to collective awakening, it points to the fact that the mystery is not only located in you, the shift in self that we experience personally must also be experienced and expressed by others. That is because our sense of self doesn't only exist in us, it is also held in the perceptions and beliefs that others hold about us. The transformative opportunity of collective awakening is to experience a dramatic shift in our sense of self, not only as it is held inside our own minds, but also in how it is held and reflected back to us from those around us. Because our transformation lives in the people around us as well as inside us, it is deeper and more stable when it happens in groups. We look inside and we see a different self, we look to the people around us and they reflect that different self back to us. I have experienced the enormously powerful benefit of this kind of mutual reinforcement. I have had profound and dramatic individual breakthroughs, but the breakthroughs of collective awakening, because they were immediately recognized by others, left a deep and unique impression on my life.

In the introduction of this book, I mentioned a dramatic experience of collective awakening that I participated in. The collective awakening or intersubjective enlightenment that occurred was a turning point in my life. There was a group of us on retreat who entered into an experience of one mind together for three weeks. Soon after the retreat I began traveling throughout the United States, Canada, Europe and Australia, in an effort to share that intersubjective awakening with as many people as I could. During all of that time and for many years after, I continued to be engaged in collective spiritual practice with others.

I taught collective awakening in different forms for twelve years, but over time I began to see that what I thought were the higher potentials of this awakening could not be realized through practice alone. I was leading dialog practice sessions that would consistently lift people into a profound experience of one mind or mutually recognized oneness. The experience was powerful enough that it left people returning repeatedly for more sessions, but the deeper realization and transformation that I knew was possible didn't seem to be happening. I have come to the conclusion that there were two primary reasons for this.

The first reason is because in order for the experience of collective awakening to result in lasting change an individual has to be ready to embrace that change. This means they are coming into the collective spiritual work having done a great deal of the kind of preparatory work that I described in the earlier chapters of this book. The second reason has to do with what we were exploring at the start of this chapter. That collective awakening is not only something that happens within an individual, it also happens within a group. Intersubjective enlightenment is not a collective awakening that happens in an individual, it is an awakening of a group or community. Each individual feels it, as long as they are connected to the others in the group. Outside of the mutually reinforcing energy of the community, the experience of collective awakening becomes a memory of something that happened to an individual.

I've had many experiences of collective awakening, but that initial experience remains the most dramatic and life changing. The circumstances of the retreat were extreme. The retreat had no set completion date, none of us knew how long we would be on retreat, but we were all committed to staying as long as it took to ignite the kind of experience we intuited was possible. In the end the retreat lasted for two months. In addition to having no end date, the retreat included a great deal of practice. By the time we would sit in our circle to engage in dialog at nine in the evening, we had been meditating since four in the morning. When we met in our dialog sessions I was not thinking about collective awakening, although that was the context for the entire retreat. All I was doing was remaining perfectly relaxed and attentive exactly as I had been all day in meditation.

In our group dialog practice sessions I would sit resting in perfect stillness, listening attentively to whatever was being said. Eventually I would feel an energetic excitement building inside me that would grow until it moved through me and emerged out of my mouth as words. From my perspective it didn't feel like I was speaking, it felt like I was watching something speak through me. When the circle was fully activated I experienced everything that was said as energy that would enter my body and sometimes trigger an energetic response in me. If I got triggered to speak, words would come out of my mouth and those words would trigger someone else to speak. Everyone was expressing themselves from a vantage point that seemed to be coming from a higher mind. I felt like a mouthpiece acting on behalf of a collective being that was having a conversation with itself. In this circumstance you speak with a depth of confidence and wisdom that you don't have when you are on your own. What emerges in that circumstance isn't necessarily a quality that you retain. At the same time, because all of us stayed in contact after the retreat, the experience did last, although less powerfully, for months, and for many of us this became the defining event of our life.

> *In relation to collective awakening, the mystery is not only located in you, the shift in self that we experience personally must also be experienced and expressed by others.*

CHAPTER ELEVEN

The Experience of Contact

ALL OF MY WORK as a writer and a teacher is dedicated to supporting people to participate in the emergence of a new possibility for humanity, by giving
birth to a new way of being, a new paradigm for human life. When doing intersubjective spiritual work,
I encourage you to embrace this context for yourself
and for whatever group you are working with. Being
driven by a desire to bring a new possibility into the
world fuels your practice and supports the possibility of deep spiritual union together. The remainder of
this book will be used to introduce a form of collective spiritual work that groups of people can engage
in together. If all of the people in the group have done
the work of deep contemplation as I have described
here, and are actively engaged in some form of practice of self-forgetting and relaxation, then the collective work they do together will yield profound results.

It is important to remember that although the
overarching context for your work is to give birth to a
new possibility for humanity, that is not a motive that

you bring directly to either your individual or collective practice. The desire to participate in a new future is what brings you to the practice, but your only focus in the practice is letting go. Whether in meditation or intersubjective dialog practices, you are relaxing into a deep sense of inner stillness and peace. Profound spiritual discovery happens in relaxation. That deep state of disengagement creates space for a different order of being to emerge. You don't move yourself into it, you relax and allow yourself to be taken in. Out of the ground of perfect stillness, another possibility begins to emerge that brings with it new feelings, intuitions and visions.

If you chase after these new perceptions they disappear and you end up back where you started. Eventually you will see that the more you relax and don't do anything, the more spiritual magic occurs. What is happening is not coming from you, you are allowing it, but you are not generating it. Spiritual practice is always about surrender. You participate in the emergence by simply relaxing and watching.

As we've already spoken about, the most important part of our practice is the release of our familiar identity through the art of self-forgetting. In practice, we give up the perspective of being a separate isolated individual and all of our tendencies toward analyzing everything from that point of view. This is crucial when doing practice and it is equally important when relating to the experiences we have afterward. When we have a powerful spiritual experience, we tend to think about it later through the familiar sense of identity. These dramatic events when they happen are overwhelming experiences not only of perceiving differently, but also perceiving from a different place. After they occur we are very likely to turn the whole event into a memory of an experience that our familiar sense of self had. It is important to avoid this tendency. Avoid thinking in an analytical way about the experiences you have - that means avoid looking through the eyes of the familiar self that wants to understand everything.

Another thing to keep in mind in doing deep spiritual work is that we don't want to hold on to any of the experiences we have or any insight we gain from them. Continued emergence requires that we remain free of ideas and open to new possibilities. We do not want to accumulate anything. The goal is to freefall through successive experiences of revelation without getting stuck in any of them. Allow the process of emergence to flow through you. There will always be a temptation to hold on to a powerful experience. To want to dwell on it, keep it present in mind, or recreate it once it fades. The only thing that you can hold onto is a memory. Real spiritual knowledge and wisdom can't be held on to like baggage. Too often we trade our direct access and immediate experience for memories that the mind can hold. You don't need to remember anything, you simply need to be relaxed, open and free. Everything else will happen all by itself.

Now I want to introduce a collective spiritual practice that I call experiencing contact. We are very familiar with the experience of contact, so familiar in fact that we don't generally even recognize it. As an intersubjective explorer of consciousness, it is important that we become deeply attuned and sensitive to the experience of contact. We have already established that we live in an intersubjective reality which means we are always in contact. Even if you are alone on a mountain top, you are in contact. The thoughts and feelings in your mind were all formed in relation to encounters with other people or circumstances. In other words, the thoughts and feelings in your mind emerge out of an intersubjective shared reality. The fact that we are always in contact is what makes it so easy for us to not notice the experience of contact, because it is always there everywhere.

The practice of experiencing contact can be done in small groups sitting in a circle, but it is actually ideal to do in pairs with two people sitting facing each other a few feet apart. The practice begins with both people sitting quietly in meditation with their eyes closed. Then at the sound of a bell they both open their eyes and continue sitting in silence looking at each other. Another bell will signal for the practitioners to close their eyes and meditate again. I recommend doing this practice for thirty minutes. You start with five minutes of meditation with eyes closed, followed by five minutes of sitting with eyes open. Repeating this cycle three times will take thirty minutes.

The purpose of this exercise is simply to notice the difference in how it feels to sit in meditation with your eyes closed and how it feels to sit looking at another person. If you pay attention you will feel a big difference, and the difference that you feel is contact. With your eyes open you are in conscious contact with another person, and it feels like something to be in contact with someone. When you do this exercise you should be just as relaxed when your eyes are open as you are when they are closed. The only thing that changes when the bell rings is that you open your eyes, and that introduces contact into your experience. When the thirty minutes of practice is over, speak in the group, or with your partner about how you experienced contact. This practice is a great warm up exercise for intersubjective dialog work that we will introduce in the next chapter.

JEFF CARREIRA

> *The desire to participate in a new future is what brings you to the practice, but your only focus in the practice is letting go.*

CHAPTER TWELVE

The Practice of Speaking from Emptiness

IN THIS CHAPTER I am going to describe a collective form of spiritual dialog practice that I call speaking from emptiness. You can think of this practice as a form of meditation in discussion. The most challenging aspect of collective spiritual work is that it depends on everyone present. The benefits of this work are tremendous, but the collective nature of it makes it supremely challenging. It is difficult for any of us individually to maintain the open-hearted innocence that allows us to be available to the unimaginable potential of collective awakening, but when working together in groups, everyone has to maintain the same wide open stance. When every person present is open something magical happens. I experienced it as a circuit of spiritual energy being created that allowed the power of awakening to flow through the group freely.

During the retreat where I experienced my first dramatic breakthrough into collective awakening, we would begin our dialog sessions just sitting in silence. There was no time limit on this period of silence. We were just sitting until someone was moved to begin speaking. Sometimes that happened after a few minutes, sometimes it took much longer, there were even times where no one ever spoke and we ended the meeting in silence. We were sitting, deeply relaxed, ready to wait as long as needed. Eventually someone would be moved to speak, and when they were, it would not be because they had thought of something they wanted to say. It would be because something wanted to speak through them. They wouldn't be speaking as much as they would be allowing something to speak. They would not know what they were going to say beforehand, they would discover what wanted to be said as it was vocalized in their mouth. Then the words would come forth. During our discussion sessions I would feel an energetic flow start to engulf the room. I would almost see it moving around the room. And then I would see it burst out as words through someone's mouth. Then those words would either trigger something in me or in someone else, and more words would be spoken. The look on everyone's face while this was happening reflected curiosity and bewilderment. No one really knew what was going to happen next, you never knew when it was going to be your turn to pop.

When you practice speaking from emptiness, you begin in silent meditation and wait until you or someone else is moved to speak. No one knows when someone will be moved to speak. You are not trying to think of something to say, and you are not looking for an inner energetic movement to stir. All you are doing is being relaxed and available. You aren't concerned with when you might speak, or if you will speak at all. Your only intention is to be completely relaxed and available and it doesn't matter if anything happens or not. You're not even hoping something will happen. You are totally satisfied just being relaxed.

In the practice of speaking from emptiness, we are meditating together, which means our focus is on being relaxed. There are two differences between this and meditating individually. One, is that in collective practice we always pay careful attention to anything anyone says. We don't think about what they say in any deliberate sense, we just listen carefully to it. The other difference is that we are open to the possibility that something will speak through us. Being open to the possibility is a passive stance. It has nothing to do with encouraging the possibility in any way. Being open to the possibility only means that we have not closed it off. We are open, that's it.

The first exercise I want to suggest is one where you sit in a group together, or in a pair, and simply wait until someone is moved to speak. When someone speaks, everyone present listens carefully. If what is said moves someone else to speak then they will speak, if not, then everyone simply falls back into silence until someone is moved to speak again. Do this for thirty minutes. It doesn't matter if nobody ever speaks. At the end of the thirty minute period talk together about what the experience was like.

Speaking from emptiness is a spoken meditation that is deeply parallel to the art of conscious contentment meditation that I teach. Speaking from emptiness is simply a meditation that we do while we are paying attention to what other people are saying, and being open that we might be moved to speak as well. The challenge of this is that it is very difficult to be sure that we are authentically moved to speak, and have not just created something to say. We might find ourselves locked in inner turmoil because we are not certain if we or anyone else is truly speaking from some place deeper than our minds. This uncertainty is inevitable. We have all been speaking from our familiar sense of self for so long, it is no big surprise that we find it difficult to speak from another source. Working through the uncertainty and all of the trial and error that it inevitably includes, is an important part of the practice. The effort we make to be clear about when we are truly speaking from emptiness is how we improve our ability to do so.

I think of the discomfort we experience doing this practice as the cosmic burning off of the habit of seeing yourself only as a separate individual. Speaking from the knowledge of your individual mind is a deep

THE MYSTERY OF COLLECTIVE AWAKENING

karmic habit, and just like with any habit, the process of breaking it is uncomfortable. If you stopped smoking cigarettes after having smoked for a long time, it would be uncomfortable. In this practice we are working against a very strong habit of speaking from what we think we know. It will be uncomfortable. We will need to make a lot of space for discomfort as we embark on this practice.

It is my sincere hope that some of the people who read this book will be inspired to explore the mystery of collective awakening so I want to end with some specific guidance for how you can do that if you feel compelled to. This work needs to be done with at least one other person, but a small group of five or six people is preferable. It is important that everyone engaged in the work has a similar understanding of what they are doing and similar intentions in doing it. I suggest that spending some time reading and discussing the ideas and perspectives presented in this book would be an excellent way to begin to generate coherence in the group. A simple way to accomplish this would be for each member in the group to read one of the chapters in this book and then gather to discuss it together. Although these will be more traditional discussions than the speaking from emptiness practice we just described, I would still recommend listening deeply and waiting until you feel moved to speak as a general guideline.

Over the time that the group is engaged in these discussions, each member should also be involved in their own individual spiritual practice. I recommend practicing meditation and if you want to follow my instructions you will find an in depth description of them in my book *The Experience of Luminous Absorption*. Each individual involved in the group practice should choose an individual practice that they feel will best support them to maintain the open availability and fluidity of identity that we've been describing as the necessary ground for intersubjective spiritual work. It is most powerful if all the members gather together to engage in a practice like meditation because doing spiritual work together develops the deep bonds of trust that are necessary for this subtle and sensitive work.

Whenever the group feels bonded in spirit and purpose around the collective work, it will be time to begin the speaking from emptiness practice. I suggest beginning with half hour sessions, once or twice a week. When these sessions begin to feel too short, you can increase the time to forty five minutes, and then an hour. I suggest not engaging in this practice for longer than ninety minutes. If you follow these guidelines I am sure that you and your fellow explorers will unleash extraordinary revelations and open up new worlds of possibility.

Many years ago I experienced a collective awakening that changed the course of my life. At that time I knew that I had experienced a miraculous appearance of a higher order being. I have had many experiences of collective awakening since and this book contains the culmination of insights that all of my experiences have led to. I believe the profound perceptual shift that occurs in the spiritual union of collective spiritual work offers a vision of future potentials that can be realized on this planet. Intersubjective spiritual work is delicate and subtle. It requires tremendous dedication and sensitivity and a wide open heart and mind. Those who feel called to this work are being called to participate in the emergence of a new way of being human and a new possibility for consciousness on the Earth.

*When every person present
maintains the open-hearted
innocence that allows us to be
available to the unimaginable
potential of collective awakening -
something magical happens.*

About the Author

JEFF CARREIRA IS A meditation teacher, mystical philosopher and author who teaches to a growing number of people throughout the world. As a teacher, Jeff offers retreats and courses guiding individuals in a form of meditation he refers to as The Art of Conscious Contentment. Through this simple and effective meditation technique, Jeff has led thousands of people in the journey beyond the confines of fear and self-concern into the expansive liberated awareness that is our true home.

Ultimately, Jeff is interested in defining a new way of being in the world that will move us from our current paradigm of separation and isolation into an emerging paradigm of unity and wholeness. He is exploring some of the most revolutionary ideas and systems of thought in the domains of spirituality, consciousness, and human development. He teaches people how to question their own experience so deeply that previously held assumptions about the nature of reality fall away to create space for dramatic shifts in understanding.

Jeff is passionate about philosophy because he is passionate about the power of ideas to shape how we perceive reality and how we live together. His enthusiasm for learning is infectious, and he enjoys addressing student groups and inspiring them to develop their own powers of inquiry. He has taught students at colleges and universities throughout the world.

Jeff is the author of numerous books including: *The Art of Conscious Contentment, No Place But Home, The Miracle of Meditation, The Practice of No Problem, Embrace All That You Are, Philosophy Is Not a Luxury, Radical Inclusivity, The Soul of a New Self,* and *Paradigm Shifting.*

For more about Jeff or to book him for a speaking engagement, visit: jeffcarreira.com

Made in the USA
Las Vegas, NV
06 November 2022

58850877R00090